CW01024490

Ostriches

Ten Poems about My Dad

Candlestick Press

Published by:
Candlestick Press,
Diversity House, 72 Nottingham Road, Arnold, Nottingham NG5 6LF
www.candlestickpress.co.uk

Design and typesetting by Craig Twigg

Printed by Bayliss Printing Company Ltd of Worksop, UK

Poems and Introduction © Jeanette Burton, 2024

Cover illustration © likovaka/Shutterstock

Candlestick Press monogram © Barbara Shaw, 2008

© Candlestick Press, 2024

ISBN 978 1 913627 40 9

Acknowledgements

'Poem in which my dad plays pool in a Spanish bar' was highly commended in
the Teignmouth Open Poetry Competition 2022 and The Plough Poetry Prize
2023. 'Poem in which my dad's ear is haunted by the ghost of Tutankhamun' was
published on the Poetry Wales website as part of a shortlisting in the Poetry
Wales Pamphlet Competition 2021. 'I contemplate the afterlife whilst watching
an episode of Only Fools and Horses with my dad' won first prize in the Poets,
Prattlers and Pandemonialists Poetry Prize 2023. 'The Importance of Being
Earnest' was published by The Friday Poem, April 12th 2024. All other poems
published here for the first time.

Contents   Page

Introduction   5

Poem in which my dad thinks Armageddon   7
is only moments away

Poem in which my dad plays pool in a Spanish bar   8 - 9

Poem in which my dad's ear is haunted by the   10
ghost of Tutankhamun

I contemplate the afterlife whilst watching an   11
episode of *Only Fools and Horses* with my dad

Ostriches   12 - 13

If you have a treasured possession that's   14 - 15
seen better days

The Importance of Being Earnest   16 - 17

Poem in which I recount the finding of my   18 - 19
dad's love letter to my mum in the style of
a Ronnie Corbett monologue

Measuring our father   20 - 21

Poem in which my dad carries things   22 - 23

Introduction

Dads are awesome fellows. In fact, they are having something of a renaissance in popular culture, thanks in no small part to Pedro Pascal's star turn as a fiercely protective father/father figure in *The Last of Us* and *The Mandalorian*. Now, my dad, as far as I know, hasn't battled mutant fungi, nor has he masqueraded as a Bounty Hunter, shielding Baby Yoda from Imperial forces in a galaxy far, far away. No, my dad, like many dads out there, is an everyman, an ordinary bloke, a working-class lad from a Derbyshire town. Nothing remarkable, but therein lie his extraordinary superpowers. Mild-mannered he may be, but when he takes a spin in his shed, he emerges in blue overalls, ready to save the world with drill and paint brush.

So, my dad is a fully-fledged superhero. And we all know that superheroes have their famous catchphrases. Robin has "holy smoke, Batman!" and my dad has "dunna wittle, it'll be reet, I'll go t'our house". The first poem in this pamphlet introduces these sayings – East Midlands dialect – which are so much part of my dad's identity. They are also the fabric of my childhood; I would hang on his every word, wanting to believe "this dad-shaped philosophy" would rescue me again and again.

Several of the poems explore the idea that our dads, like superheroes, are infinite. If only we could take them to *The Repair Shop* to be fixed, or watch beloved sitcoms on repeat, to find them reincarnated as the same people. Alas, even Superman has his kryptonite.

The latter poems show a more adult perspective. As my dad would say, "at the end of the day, when you've done and said all", fathers are gloriously human in all their flawed brilliance. Our dads may be mere mortals, but to know them, "we look to the stars".

Jeanette Burton

Poem in which my dad thinks Armageddon is only moments away

When I was a small child, my dad lived in a perpetual
state of shock, so that everything had the weight

of an asteroid hitting the earth or the moon zipping
off into space. *Well, I'll go t'foot of our stairs*, he'd say,

then, *I'll go t'our house*, but not for life-or-death situations.
No, just if the dog turned his nose up at his breakfast

or if one of the hanging baskets fell off the garden shed.
His shock would soon subside to *dunna wittle, it'll be reet*,

like he'd suddenly realised an apocalypse was doubtful,
even if he had found a handprint on a freshly painted door,

or that the four-minute warning was increasingly unlikely
in the event of a split hose. Still, I wondered how it helped

to go to the foot of our stairs. What was there? The chance
to take stock? The opportunity to rationalise the outrage?

Were the first two steps more soothing than the middle
or the top? I couldn't fathom it, but now, when I'm brought

to a state of shock, I'll go to our house, to the foot of our stairs.
And although an asteroid could be hurtling towards us,

although we may only have seconds left, I wait for my dad
to sit beside me, whisper in my ear, *dunna wittle, it'll be reet*.

Poem in which my dad plays pool in a Spanish bar

He paces and pivots around the shabby table,
ripped green baize willowing the worn cushions.

He's channelling Steve Davis, as if instead of shorts
and T-shirt, he's dressed in waistcoat and dickie.

He's eyeing the black ball – its 8 reduced to 6
from years of rough play – weighing it up,

like he does a DIY job back at home, the best way
to approach it. He pauses, chalks the flattened tip,

allows the cue to leisurely lean against his shoulder
like a confidante. He calculates the shot, an angle,

spreads half his body across the table, right leg
thrust out, stubbled chin grazing smooth maple.

His eyes flick from cue to ball, cue to ball, cue to
wife, son, daughter, watching in the semi-darkness.

He strikes, sends the white thundering towards
the black, smacks it so hard it jumps clean out

of the pocket. My brother is determined to catch it,
but it meteorites the wooden decking, rolls across

the floor before finally coming to rest between
my frilly socked and plastic sandaled five-year-old feet.

There you go, kiddo, he says, *you can't win 'em all.*
It's a phrase he returns to when things don't work out:

ballet classes, driving tests, haircuts, exams, love.
I assumed this dad-shaped philosophy would be enough

to ward off the disappointments of every setback.
I tried to conjure up the black ball soaring through air,

its bid for freedom, but for years I could only remember
what happened next: the white ball making its slow

and deliberate progress towards the middle pocket.
Its smooth drop, like fresh milk poured into a jug.

Now, when I think of the losses, those near-misses,
I prefer my dad's retelling of events: the epic flight,

black ball as unlikely superhero, blazing a trail above
the heads of my family, locals, bar staff, holidaymakers,

all stunned into silence by this strange leap of faith.

Poem in which my dad's ear is haunted by the ghost of Tutankhamun

He announced it shortly after tea one weekday evening.
The doctors couldn't find a logical explanation for it,
no formal diagnosis forthcoming, no sign of infection,
no glue ear, no need for syringing, no apparent hearing loss,
antihistamines for out-of-season hay fever proved fruitless.
So it was that this strange tinnitus was labelled a visitation –
Tutankhamun's spirit had hitched a ride inside my dad's ear,
curled genie-like into his ear canal, coiled itself around
the cochlea, for no other reason than to send him near mad
with buzzing, whistling, the sense of being submerged in water.
This certainly wasn't the first time his body had been possessed
by a King of Egypt. No, this curse was long standing, a pharaoh
had been squatting in my dad's head since my parents visited
Luxor for their 25th wedding Anniversary. Then, it spooked
with panic attacks, a racing heartbeat, bouts of depression.
This most definitely wasn't the result of sudden redundancy,
dad said, or the textile industry moving to a foreign country,
or starting again after thirty years of working his way up.
It was in no way caused by having to learn the world anew,
months of applications, interviews, psychometric testing -
only to be told, *you were very close, it came down to two,*
but in the end the other candidate just pipped you to the post.
No, it was none of these things, it was Tutankhamun and his tricks.
I had my doubts, we all did, but it didn't stop me from booking
a holiday to Egypt last Spring. I followed in my parent's footsteps,
cruised the Nile, accompanied other tourists on a dawn coach trip
to the Valley of Kings. I inched my way down the steep corridors
to his famous tomb and standing before the tiny sarcophagus
of a dead teenager, I held my hands together as if in prayer.
I whispered: *I want my dad back. Please get out of his ear.*

I contemplate the afterlife whilst watching an episode of *Only Fools and Horses* with my dad

Rodney is telling Del Boy that if he ends up being reincarnated,
it would be just his luck to come back as himself and I can't help
but think about this one duck I encountered in the park last week.
She opened her beak and out came, not a quack, but Sid James'
laugh and it occurs to me that maybe we don't come back
as ourselves, maybe it's just our best bits, our lovable parts
passed on to someone or something, so that somewhere
in the world is a cat with the comic timing of Tommy Cooper,
or a little girl with the homing instincts of a prize Carrier pigeon.
My dad wheezes out his almost silent laugh, as he always does
when he watches classic comedy and I wonder if after he's gone
this will transfer to the soul of an antelope or a ballet dancer.
What if my dad's best traits are not his at all, but actually belong
to a sheep farmer from New Zealand, a chocolatier from France?
What if in a past life my dad was a squadron leader from WW2?
How would we ever know? I doubt this pilot had celebrity status.
He wasn't famous, no Sid James or your run of the mill reincarnation:
Henry VIII, Elvis, the captain of the Titanic. But one day there could be
a child, a daughter, who bumps into my dad, knows how to separate
man from man, tells us all about her father's farewell smile,
(which we always thought unique to our dad), how he beamed
at his waving children every time he set off on dangerous mission.
What if this man had no family, no friends, shunned human contact?
What if no one came after, no one to stop my dad in the street,
say, *you'll never believe this, but you are the absolute spit of my
father, grandfather, godfather, uncle ...?* Then we'd never know
if our annual holidays abroad, planned like a military procedure,
were our dad's design or a throwback to the mid nineteenth century.
Back in Nelson Mandela House, the Trotter brothers are busy plotting
another scheme and hoping to be millionaires by this time next year.
I look over at my dad who wheezes at Uncle Albert's *during the war...*
If Rodney's right about the afterlife, if I'm reincarnated as myself,
I'll get to relive these moments with my dad, watching 80s sitcoms,
even if he sneezes like an Arctic explorer, sings like a Welsh miner,
if like a great compilation clip, he's made of the best bits from before.

Ostriches

Friday afternoon and I'm driving my dad
to the Ford garage in Derby to pick up his car.
It's strange to have him in the passenger seat,
never one to be chauffeured, only ever playing
sidekick when he granted me a few lessons

as a teenager. We bickered endlessly on those
fraught Sunday mornings, navigating snaky
country lanes in a foul tempered stupor, my dad
thrusting out a foot to find a phantom brake,
bracing for impact at every light, every junction.

He only marvelled at my expert clutch control,
something he still brings up at family gatherings:
Oh, that girl is a genius with a biting point! Today,
I can sense him watching me, judging my ability
to handle this motor, and I feel like a learner

again, not sure when to change gear, trying to do
everything correctly, mirror, signal, manoeuvre.
I can see his eyes move from speedometer to
wing mirrors, to gear stick and it occurs to me
that he never really looks out of the window,

has never really had chance to take in the view.
Back when we took long car journeys to far-flung
places like Swanage and Rhyl, my dad always
claimed the wheel, a classic 80s formation:
father at the helm, captain, calmly steering

the ship, mother, first officer, designated map
reader, kids stowed in the back. While we passed
the time playing eye spy with cows, sheep, pylons,
emergency telephones, a Happy Eater restaurant,
my dad focused on the road ahead or turned briefly

to shout, *give it a rest, you pair! Stop tip tapping!*
Then, with the absence of DVDs or social media,
me and my brother gave thumbs up to lorry drivers,
tallying the friendly responses, excited in competition,
extra points for a wave or the sounding of a horn.

And still dad looked straight ahead, never tired,
just a quick pitstop for a ham cob, flask of coffee.
Now, sat beside me, he's missing out again,
fiddling with the air conditioning, obsessed with
locating a mysterious rattle. I point and say, *dad,*

look, there's ostriches in the field over there.
He finally looks, really looks, sees this swagger
of flightless birds taking in the world around them,
the fence, the road, the cars, the people inside,
the pair of us, here, watching something beautiful.

If you have a treasured possession that's seen better days

bring it along to the *Repair Shop*. We rummage
for heirlooms, find dad gathering dust on the sofa,
take him off to the famous barn where Jay Blades
greets us with a nod and a gold-toothed grin.

We tell him dad was made in December 1946,
not rare, one of many in production after WW2.
Baby Boomer model, says my mum, *white male,
part of the Working-Class line, typical of the era.*

Mum goes on to say she acquired him in the sixties
and he's been in the family ever since. Originally,
he came with accessories, a self-taught edition:
paint brush, drill, ladder, tape measure, sander,

saw, screwdriver, three sheds. *Some have been
lost*, says my brother, *but he's still got his voice box
with all the sayings we've played over and over.*
We listen to some of them now. *Well, I'll go t'foot*

of our stairs! It's muck or nettles. Dunna wittle!
Years of usage have revealed him to be durable,
guaranteed non-stop play value and functionality,
programmed to mend, to build, to dig, to carry,

to earn, to joke, to drive, to laugh, to tinker, to love.
What would you like us to do for him? A moment's
pause, before we decide a little spruce is enough.
Horologist, Steve, marvels at what makes him tick,

top notch mechanism, just a few screws to tighten.
Dad keeps excellent time, has never once been late,
a quirk of British manufacture. The Bear Ladies
patch up his blue overalls, give him a fresh shock

of black hair, replace the padding around his limbs
so he no longer hobbles or stumbles when he walks.
Susie, an expert in leather, oils, polishes, buffs
and scuffs his skin until the olive hue is restored.

Metal worker, Dom, tucks a newly crafted toolbox
under our father's arm, covers him in a sheet
for the final reveal. When we see dad again,
we whoop at the transformation. *It's remarkable!*

He's just like we remember from thirty years ago!
Will, the carpenter, has made a display cabinet
to keep him safe, but dad's off, down the gravel path,
reaching for the spanner, wondering what to fix next.

The Importance of Being Earnest

There in the audience, my mother and me,
lights yet to be dimmed, unwrapping

Starburst, getting the rustling over before
the start, the curtains opening, the actors

taking centre stage. That's when we spot him.
My dad. Or more precisely, my dad's double,

same profile, greying hair, blue bomber jacket.
Look! That chap is the absolute spit of your dad!

Because there's no way it's him. He doesn't
have a ticket, only ever offers to play taxi driver,

giving us a lift, then snoozing in the car or sloping
off to McDonald's for a double cheeseburger.

If it's not him, it's his doppelganger or his ghost,
my mum whispers with a note of real concern

in her voice and I think of *The X-Files* episode,
the one where Scully sees her father before

the phone call to tell her he's dead. We examine
this man, this imposter father in the stalls,

until, finally he turns, smiles and waves up to us.
It is dad! we exclaim, breathing a sigh of relief.

Too cold to wait in the car, he tells us afterwards,
decided to get himself a ticket in the third row.

We laugh, but then I think of the future, near,
far, whenever, watching another Wilde,

in another theatre where I will see him again,
in the circle, or up in the gods, and I will want

him to turn, smile, wave down to me forever.

Poem in which I recount the finding of my dad's love letter to my mum in the style of a Ronnie Corbett monologue

Tonight, I want to tell you a completely new story. Now, now. Don't be like that. I'm not going to repeat the legendary tale of the night my dad accused one of the neighbours of skulduggery when he saw him innocently climb atop his outhouse to gain a better view of the blood red supermoon. It's not even the one about the time my dad got us up so early to go on holiday that we arrived before the airport had been built. This one starts with a letter. No, no, not the letters I get every week asking me, for the love of God, get to the point. No, not that kind of letter or the other kind (the less said about them the better...) No, this is a letter sent by my dad to my mum when they were courting in the late sixties. A love letter. *Should you be reading that out?* I hear one person in the audience cry out. Let me reassure you, madam. There is nothing remotely racy about this letter. In fact, it has the same tone as the letter he wrote to *Points of View* when *Howard's Way* became a regular feature on Sunday nights. Indeed, slightly less emotional. I should, at this point in proceedings, make you aware that my dad is with us this evening. Oh yes, he is somewhere out there in the darkness, no doubt reluctant and definitely disgruntled that he has been dragged away from whatever project it is that he is working on. He once earned himself the nickname 'Caractacus Potts', Dick Van Dyke's character in *Chitty Chitty Bang Bang*. He was always inventing things that didn't quite work. Still, after every two-month stint of redesigning the garage, we always expected him to emerge pipping the horn of a flying car. Anyway, I digress. And so, to the letter, which I found in a suitcase in the loft, alongside an old vinyl copy of *Rubber Soul*, a plastic spade minus its bucket and an ornate photograph album. I might add that my discovery also included many blurry snaps of unidentifiable landscapes, several shots of my family missing feet and scalps and the rest quite rightly labelled 'quality control'. Anyway, back to the story. My dad's love letter. It is important to note the singularity of this note. I did not discover a bundle of envelopes faintly scented with perfume and tied together with a red ribbon. No, just the one solitary love letter. I have it with me tonight and I'll read you the opening lines. *Dear Andrea, I hope you had a lovely time on your holiday to Ilfracombe.* Now, as you can imagine with such a tantalising start, I was eager to devour the rest of the contents, be witness to my parents' burgeoning romance, my dad's declaration of love, his, *oh, how I have missed you, my darling! Please don't leave again! Not even for one minute!* This is what actually came next: *I've been wondering all week if you arrived at the caravan on time? I noticed there were road works on Bridge Street. I hope you didn't get caught up in them. Always give yourself that extra half hour.* Ladies and gentleman, boys and girls, I'm sure you'll want to join me in giving a warm round of applause to my dad, the Cyrano de Bergerac of traffic congestion. He'll want to wish you all a safe journey home. Wait a minute. What's that? He's left already? Wanted to avoid rush hour? Left me a handwritten note in my dressing room? Dad, you've missed the punchline.

Measuring our father

At first, hardwired by ancestry,
we worked in approximations:
cups of tea consumed
whilst fixing our BMX bikes,
days he spent in the shed
building a wooden sledge,
trips to the tip, to the seaside,
repeated readings of *Mr Tickle*.
Spurred on by ancient Egyptians,
we looked to the land,
designed our own Dadometer,
gauged his sway on the seasons:
summers he mowed the lawn,
winters he tidied the garden.
We navigated his movements
by the heavens, the sun low
in the sky when he washed the car,
the moon a waning gibbous
when he set off for a night shift.
School brought standardisation,
protractors, rulers, metric.
We abandoned estimation,
embraced accuracy,
the exactitude of his age,
his weight, his height.
We synchronised Casio watches,
always knew the precise time
he arrived home from work,
the number of hours
he wanted to be at the airport
before the plane took off.
Later, we quibbled over benchmarks,
found inconsistent calculations,
his behaviour not quite adding up.
If our future predictions are correct,
precision is what will be required,

his life measured in boxes.
For now, we return to the old ways,
before the bath, before *Eureka!*
We look to the stars.

Poem in which my dad carries things

He carried himself downstairs every morning
for over thirty years, precisely 6am, setting off
with his snap box to carry out his job at the Mill.

As a boy, he carried bags of chips, a football
to the local park, a wrench to his father fixing
a car in the yard. Entering the world of work

at fifteen, he carried a lamp down Ormande pit,
then above ground, a torch to check machinery
at Blounts Hosiery Factory. Just twenty-one,

he carried his father's coffin, a plate of biscuits
to a small group of family carrying their grief.
Thirty, he carried toiletries and fresh nightgowns

to his mother in the nursing home. Early forties,
he carried buckets of water when the garage
flooded, bedding plants, a hand-made sledge,

suitcases, a tape measure, fish from the fair,
a ladder. Mid-fifties, he carried rolls of wallpaper
to his son's new house, his first granddaughter

in her car seat. Now retired, he carries a bowl
of cornflakes to his quiet corner of the room
where he reads the news, clicks through emails.

Outside, he carries an assortment of tools to
and from the shed; a power drill, a screwdriver,
a hammer. In the evening, he carries cups of tea

to his daughter, his wife, both watching soaps.
At night, he carries himself off to bed, weary,
heavy, like he is weighing his own aged bones,

like he is carrying an extra person, as he did,
all those years ago when he carried me upstairs,
read to me, letting his voice carry me off to sleep.